Original title:
Boughs and Ballads

Copyright © 2025 Creative Arts Management OÜ
All rights reserved.

Author: Seraphina Caldwell
ISBN HARDBACK: 978-1-80567-317-0
ISBN PAPERBACK: 978-1-80567-616-4

Chants from the Forest Floor

In the woods, where critters prance,
Fungi joke, and squirrels dance.
Frogs croak tunes in harmony,
Nature's choir, full of glee.

Leaves drop down with gentle flair,
Tickling birds that float in air.
A rabbit laughs, a deer makes way,
All nature's jokes on display!

The Rhythm of Rustling Leaves

Whispers travel with the breeze,
Rustling tales from moonlit trees.
An acorn slips and starts to roll,
Making friends with the woodland mole.

Each leaf shakes with a giddy cheer,
Singing loudly for all to hear.
The branches sway with laughter bright,
A merry dance through the night!

Chronicles of the Twisted Trunks

Twisted trunks with stories told,
Of funny critters, brave and bold.
A raccoon wears a hat of pine,
While setting up a dinner line.

One tree bends and it starts to groan,
Complaining of the weight it's grown.
Another giggles, sways with pride,
As squirrels gather nuts inside!

Anthems of the Aged Oak

Old grandfather oak stands so wise,
Cracking jokes about the skies.
His branches stretch and seem to sway,
In rhythm with the skies so gray.

The younger trees blush with delight,
As he spins tales of ancient night.
A spider weaves a laughing thread,
While whispers of the past are spread!

Sonnet of the Serene Glade

In a glade where squirrels plot their schemes,
Grass tickles toes in fuzzy, green dreams.
A bird sneezed loud and startled the fawn,
While raccoons dance under the blush of dawn.

With acorns flying like tiny, round bombs,
Each creature laughing, avoiding tree palms.
The owls hoot jokes, their wisdom aglow,
As sunlight spills secrets the mushrooms know.

Whispers of the Woodland Spirits

The whispers rustle like leaves in the air,
As chipmunks giggle without a care.
A fox tells tales of the cats who roam,
While crickets compose their nightly poem.

A deer wears glasses, a scholar by night,
Reciting sonnets with great delight.
The breeze plays a tune, a playful refrain,
Causing daisies to dance in the rain.

Reveries Among the Bark

In a forest where trees wear coats of thick bark,
A woodpecker's laugh echoes bright in the dark.
The mushrooms gossip, their caps all aflame,
While snails draft letters that nobody claims.

With shadows that tumble and frolic around,
Each twig has a tale that escapes with a sound.
A hedgehog's quiff, fashionably wild,
Makes even the shiest of critters feel riled.

Harmonious Hues of Nature

Colors collide where the wildflowers grow,
A rainbow of giggles set free with a blow.
Bees buzz in rhythm, a jazzy parade,
While butterflies boast of their glittering blades.

The sun dabs its paint on each cheek of the glen,
As laughter erupts from the chorus of men.
With frogs in the choir, croaking their part,
It's nature's own symphony, straight from the heart.

Nymphs of the Natural Nest

In the trees, where giggles grow,
Nymphs with acorns put on a show.
Swinging high on leafy ropes,
They trade their tales, their dreams, their hopes.

Squirrels join in, a tap-dancing crew,
Flipping nuts and sharing their stew.
Laughter echoes under the sun,
In this merry place, all have fun.

Poetic Bark

A tree once dreamed of being a bard,
With leafy pages, it strummed so hard.
Its bark was rough, but words flowed smooth,
Nature's rhythms made all hearts groove.

Each gust of wind would whisper a tune,
As squirrels collaborated with the moon.
Chirps from birds and rustles from grass,
Nature's concert, come one, come all, come pass!

Chromatic Chorus of the Canopies

In the heights, colors clash in cheer,
Who would have thought they'd make such a weird,
A redbird croons, a bluejay grins,
Together they start, and chaos begins!

The leaves sway, dance with delight,
As colors unite in wild flight.
Grasshoppers bring the beats, oh so grand,
A riot of hues, a fun-loving band!

The Secret Life of Saplings

Tiny sprouts with secrets to share,
Whispering jokes in sunlight's glare.
Their roots intertwine, making a pact,
To hide from the bunnies, and that's a fact!

Under the moon, they plot their play,
Cartwheeling leaves, oh what a display!
In their world, the tallest tales soar,
Secret life, oh how they explore!

Whispers in the Canopy

Up in the trees, the squirrels play,
Chasing their tails, in a dance, hooray!
With acorns flying through the air,
Who knew that nuts could cause such flair?

Birds gossip loudly about the breeze,
Sharing their secrets with great ease,
While woodpecker drums a funny beat,
Nature's circus on my street.

Melodies of the Old Oak

The old oak sings with creaky tunes,
Barking out jokes beneath the moons,
It's got a trunk that's big and round,
With punchlines buried safe and sound.

Each branch sways like a jolly mime,
Tickling the leaves with its sense of rhyme,
Squirrels giggle as they flip and twirl,
In this wacky woodland, it's quite a whirl.

Lullabies Beneath the Leaves

Under the foliage, the critters snooze,
Dreaming of cheeseburgers and funny shoes,
In a world where chips fly high and free,
And every tree's a jester, can't you see?

Rabbits hum tunes of escape and prank,
While the raccoons plot from their leafy bank,
Each lullaby wraps the night in cheer,
With giggles and rustles for all to hear.

Echoes from the Branches

Echoes come back from afar, like jokes,
Riddles bouncing, teasing the folks,
A wise old owl hoots a punchline crude,
While frogs croak laughter, oh so rude!

The branches sway in a jovial jest,
Each leaf a player in this forest fest,
Gnarled roots rumble with drama and glee,
In this arboreal show, come laugh with me!

Musings of Moss and Mist

In the shade of the trees, I found a hat,
Made of leaves and a cheeky old cat.
He purred a tune, a curious song,
Sipping dew drops, all day long.

The squirrels held a party, all dressed in twine,
They danced around in a merry line.
With acorn snacks and wild berry wine,
Oh, the mischief they had, purely divine!

The wind told secrets, in a rush and a swirl,
Caught the tail of a butterfly, spun in a whirl.
The moss giggled softly, underfoot green,
As frogs croaked in rhythm, a jovial scene.

The sun peeped in with a cheeky grin,
Whispered to the flowers, "Let's all begin!"
With jigs and with jests, the day skipped away,
In this whimsical grove, where joy loves to play.

Cadence through the Clearing

In the glade where shadows prance,
A wiggly worm took a chance.
He led a conga line, oh so bold,
With ants and toads, such stories told.

A butterfly juggling was quite the sight,
Dropping fruit snacks, oh what delight!
They shared a chuckle, and off they spun,
Chasing the shadows, just for fun.

The owls, wise and slightly absurd,
Sipped herbal tea while they sat and heard.
Of tales from the breeze, they giggled in cheer,
Every word whispered, a riddle quite dear.

As daylight faded, the laughter soared,
Creatures of all kinds danced and roared.
Night draped its blanket, star-studded and wide,
In the merry clearing, where giggles reside.

Odes to the Hidden Hollow

In a hollow so snug, where the wild things roam,
A hedgehog wore pajamas, a spiky big dome.
He read a good book by a flickering light,
While crickets recited, their songs in the night.

A badger brewed coffee, with two scoops of sass,
Said, "Join the fun, life's too quick to pass!"
With cups overflowing and laughter so bold,
The critters exchanged their best stories retold.

The fireflies twinkled, a starry brigade,
While frogs debated on who'd serenade.
Their croaks made a symphony, funny and bright,
As the moon took a peek, through the leaves' gentle light.

The wind carried giggles, like whispers in air,
With moments so silly that banished despair.
In the hidden hollow, where joy takes its flight,
Life's a merry dance, every day and night.

The Essence of Evergreen

Among the evergreens, there's mischief afoot,
A raccoon plays tricks from his favorite root.
He juggled some pinecones, slipped on his tail,
And caused such a ruckus, the others all wail.

The owls, perched high, let out jovial hoots,
While a chipmunk adorned in a gray pair of boots.
They planned a parade, with oddball attire,
Marching in circles, inspired by fire.

A squirrel recited his best limerick page,
About nuts gone missing, a humorous stage.
With laughter erupting, the forest awoke,
In a symphony vibrant, the trees gently spoke.

The day became legend, a tale to retell,
Of the merry creatures who laughed oh so well.
In the essence of evergreen, joy weaved its thread,
With smiles in the woodlands, where fun's never dead.

Chants Above the Forest Floor

In the leafy embrace, a squirrel sings,
While a raccoon dances, with shiny things.
A llama in jive, kicks up its hooves,
While chipmunks cheer, grooving in grooves.

The branches sway, like a funky beat,
Each critter joins in, to move their feet.
A frog with a crown croaks out a rhyme,
And the butterflies twirl, lost in the time.

Rhythms of the Rustling Winds

The winds whisper secrets, a giggle or two,
As leaves tumble down, in a waltz just for you.
A porcupine hums, with a prickly voice,
While shadows of squirrels in twirlings rejoice.

A breeze tickles branches, laughter it steals,
As hedgehogs join in with their soft, squeaky reels.
The air is alive, with a comical sway,
As the forest hosts parties, by night and by day.

Tales Woven in Twigs

A wise old owl shares his quirky lore,
Of a duck who wore socks at the river's shore.
With tales of a kite that could never fly,
And a goat with a dream to reach for the sky.

In branches and twigs, these stories unfold,
Of a cat who stole fish, very brazen and bold.
As the sun dips low, snickering trees,
Whisper goofy legends in the warm evening breeze.

The Ballad of the Wandering Breeze

Through meadows of laughter, the breeze does prance,
It tickles the daisies, igniting a dance.
A lizard in shades, wearing sunglasses cool,
Says, "Join in the fun! Let's break every rule!"

With every gust, mischief it brings,
Making critters giggle, and jump with their swings.
From treetop to brook, harmony free,
The wandering gust is the life of the spree.

Portraits of Petals and Pine

In the garden, roses grin,
Holding secrets deep within.
Daisies dance in silly socks,
Playing tag around the rocks.

Pines are whispering to the breeze,
Telling tales of giggling bees.
Sunflowers wear their shades quite proud,
Joining in with a laughing crowd.

The meadow's a show of vibrant flair,
Bouncing beetles, beyond compare.
Silly squirrels on a treasure hunt,
Hiding acorns, oh, what a stunt!

Every leaf has a joke to share,
Tickling roots without a care.
Nature's chuckle, bright and loud,
Painting smiles upon the crowd.

Songs of the Silvan Spirits

Underneath the leafy arch,
Gnomes are planning quite a march.
With mushrooms caps and tiny shoes,
They tap-dance, sing, and share the blues.

Elves are juggling acorns round,
As fairies giggle, hearts unbound.
Woodland critters join in glee,
Singing songs of jubilee.

Crickets chirp with great delight,
Sending echoes into the night.
Owls wear glasses, wise and neat,
Chiming in with a rhythmic beat.

Each tree sways, a playful play,
As whispers twirl and drift away.
The woods alive with jokes and cheer,
A symphony for all to hear.

Tales from the Twisted Thicket

In thickets deep, where shadows run,
Rabbits boast of all their fun.
They flip and flop, they race like fools,
Avoiding traps and silly rules.

Snares are just for mischief's scheme,
As hedgehogs chase a golden dream.
Tales unfold of wild, wild days,
Where laughter echoes through the maze.

Foxes run with a funny flair,
Telling jokes without a care.
Underbrush is their comedy stage,
Crafting tales from age to age.

Leaves are tickling grass below,
As antics burst in a bright show.
Nature's stage, with joy, it brims,
In the thicket, fun never dims.

The Woods' Secret Symphony

In the heart of the enchanted glade,
Woodpeckers join a grand parade.
With tapping beats and chirping rhymes,
They share their jokes through the times.

A raccoon brings a shiny trick,
While frogs leap in with a quirky lick.
The trees sway, laughing in the breeze,
Rustling leaves with giggles and wheezes.

Each brook bubbles with merry tunes,
Carrying tales from the laughing moon.
Crickets chirp with rhythm and grace,
In this secret, whimsical space.

The woods resound, a joyful place,
With silly sounds that bring a smile to face.
Celebrate nature with heart and whim,
In this lively, musical hymn.

Amulets of the Ancient Arbor

In the shade of an oak sat a wise old bird,
He told silly jokes, though few heard a word.
The squirrels would laugh, with acorns they'd toss,
While the grumpy tree bark mumbled, 'What's loss?'

A rabbit then hopped by, tripping on roots,
He slipped and he slid with his oversized boots.
The wise old bird chuckled, 'You've got style, my friend!'

As the laughter of trees rang out, without end.

The Forest's Found Song

Amidst the tall trunks a chorus took flight,
With frogs as the soloists, singing at night.
A hedgehog played drums on a fallen old log,
While fireflies danced, turning moonlight to fog.

The critters all jammed under twinkling stars,
Chirping tunes that rang like nonsensical bars.
A raccoon with a tambourine joined the fun,
As the leaves clapped along till the rise of the sun.

Resonance of Rain-kissed Roots

When raindrops fell down on the earth's leafy toes,
A chorus erupted from damp, happy rows.
With a croak and a squeak, the critters all cheered,
For no one was sad, and nobody feared.

The snails slid in sync, making tracks in the mud,
While a worm pulled a face, looking quite like a dud.
But laughter erupted, a joy uncontained,
As roots tapped along, completely unchained.

The Enchanted Ensemble

In a grove where the giggles grew tall as the trees,
Lived a troupe of odd critters, all buzzing with glee.
A parrot told tales, and a fox danced around,
While turtles played maracas—they made quite a sound!

With a wiggle and jiggle, they paraded with flair,
As a caterpillar crooned, causing all to stare.
The woods were alive with their comical show,
In a musical magic that few critters know.

Stories from the Shimmering Shade

Underneath the leafy dome,
A squirrel claims his throne of foam.
With acorns stacked in silly towers,
He calls them all his rightful power.

The sunbeams dance and play around,
As tiny bugs begin to sound.
A ladybug starts telling jokes,
While ants all laugh like silly folks.

A bird sings out a comic tune,
While frogs join in, you'd think it's noon!
Whiskered critters, plump and round,
All join the fun, the laughter's found.

The shade grows thick, the stories swell,
With hiccups from an owl's happy yell.
In laughter wraps this leafy glade,
Such stories bloom in joyful shade.

Hymns of the Heartwood

In the woods where tall trees sway,
A woodpecker has much to say.
He taps a beat, so rhythmically,
Announcing tunes so sprightly and free.

A chipmunk joins with clumsy steps,
As other creatures laugh with hefts.
Their chubby cheeks, with nuts they hoard,
In rhythmic jest, they can't afford.

A deer prances, slips, and trips,
Then giggles out through twitching lips.
The chorus of mischief fills the air,
Each sound a song, beyond compare.

The heartwood hums in whispered delight,
As shadows dance, both day and night.
The creatures tease, their spirits light,
In this grand hymn, they take their flight.

Whispers of the Canopy

The leaves are chatty up so high,
They gossip breezy, oh my, oh my!
A parrot squawks in vibrant tones,
Revealing secrets on wooden bones.

A sloth rumbles with a sleepy grin,
He mumbles tales of where he's been.
The monkeys swing and steal the show,
With antics brighter than a rainbow.

The sunlight filters through the green,
Creating sketches, bright and keen.
Their laughter echoes through the air,
As whispered words dance without a care.

The canopy hums a breezy note,
A symphony on a playful boat.
With every rustle, joy and cheer,
In every whisper, laughter's near.

Songs Under the Arbor

Beneath the arch of leafy might,
A rabbit hops to join the light.
He sings a song of silly dreams,
As playful sunlight twinkles and beams.

A turtle pops its head with flair,
And joins the rabbit without a care.
They dance around, such clumsy feet,
In every twirl, the joy's replete.

The vines twist tight in giggling glee,
As wiggly worms hum melodies.
A fox with style jumps in too,
Creating chaos, happy crew!

Under the bower, life's a show,
With every note, the fun will flow.
They sing of nothing, yet of each,
A melody we all can teach.

Enchanted Echoes in the Glade

In the glade where whispers play,
A squirrel danced the night away.
He lost his nut in frolic glee,
Now it's a game of hide and see.

The flowers giggle as they bloom,
While crickets plan a late-night stew.
A rabbit hops with shoes too tight,
Tripping over roots, oh what a sight!

The moon peeks in with cheeky light,
As shadows jiggle, spry and bright.
A wise old owl gives quite the show,
With jokes that only creatures know.

The breeze is filled with laughter's sway,
As frogs partake in their ballet.
They croak their tunes, a merry lot,
In nature's concert, smiles are caught.

Rhymes of the Rising Saplings

Small saplings stretch, so tall, so spry,
They compete to touch the sky.
A sunflower trips and makes a fuss,
Saying, "I'm the tallest, look at us!"

The moss below starts to dispute,
Claiming it's king, while grass shouts "Suit!"
They argue how to sway and dance,
In nature's silly, merry prance.

A berry bush with whispers sly,
Says, "Let's form a band! Oh my!"
The thorns strum tunes full of zest,
While bees provide the buzzing jest.

A whirlwind sets the scene ablaze,
As leaves twirl like in a craze.
With laughter echoing through the night,
They sing their rhymes 'til morning light.

Melodies at Twilight's Gate

At twilight's gate, the stars parade,
While owls croon in leafy shade.
The fireflies flash their tiny lights,
Dancing in such joyful flights.

A hedgehog hums a ballad sweet,
With a shuffle and a little beat.
The trees join in with rustling hands,
While the moon smiles on their bands.

Squirrels gossip on the wire,
Trading tales that never tire.
"Who stole my acorn?" one does fret,
"No one knows, and that's the bet!"

Amidst the giggles, breezes waltz,
While shadows winkle with flying faults.
A chorus born in nature's sway,
Will serenade the night away.

The Chorus of the Woodland

In woodland realms where laughter rings,
A chorus of nature hums and sings.
The trees sway with a twist and twirl,
As leaves play tag in a joyful whirl.

A badger dons a silly hat,
While singing sweet to a purring cat.
They jig in circles around a stone,
Making merry, never alone.

The brook joins in with bubbly cheer,
Tickling toes that draw near.
A toad joins with a trumpet loud,
While insects form the perfect crowd.

Each note a giggle, each beat a smile,
Nature's antics go on for miles.
As twilight nudges down the day,
The woodland chorus laughs and plays.

Serenade of the Setting Sun

A squirrel strums on a twig so wide,
Chasing shadows, he's a nutcase with pride.
The sun dips low in a wink and a grin,
While crickets join in, let the fun begin!

A raccoon waltzes, all fancy and spry,
Twisting and turning, oh my, oh my!
With fireflies buzzing like tiny flashlights,
They dance in a whirl, igniting the nights.

Sagas of the Swaying Trees

A tree with a hat, what a sight to behold,
Whispers of laughter, stories untold.
Leaves give a chuckle; they rustle in glee,
While branches jive to a tune, 'Here's a bee!'

The acorns gossip, the pinecones dare,
Swinging on breezes like dancers in air.
And every old oak has a joke to share,
As the winds weave warmth in the cool evening air.

Harmonies of the Hidden Grove

In a glade where the daisies wear smiles so wide,
A hedgehog sings softly, with friends by his side.
The mushrooms all cheer with their tops pointing high,
As ladybugs twirl on a leaf's lullaby.

The owl hoots rhythm as night takes the stage,
Raccoon with a tambourine, he's quite the sage.
A jumble of critters, they join in the spree,
Echoing tales of the fun they see.

The Song of Knotted Roots

The roots play hopscotch, all knotted and neat,
While chipmunks serenade with tiny heartbeats.
Frogs are the backup with croaks full of cheer,
Underneath the branches, the laughter is clear.

Each twist and each turn, a comical plot,
With snapshots of mischief, a bluesy thought.
The path is a melody, a dance on the floor,
Where siblings of nature forever encore!

Serenades of the Swaying Trees

The branches dance with quirky style,
Leaves giggle softly all the while.
Squirrels join with a jump and a twirl,
Chasing each other in a leafy whirl.

A crow sings out, just off-key,
While raccoons tap on trunks with glee.
The wind whispers jokes that make them sway,
Nature's band plays on, come what may.

Mushrooms nod, turning bright with delight,
As shadows chuckle with all their might.
A woodpecker joins, with a peck, peck, peck,
Creating rhythms from trunk to neck.

So, join the fun in this leafy fest,
Where laughter lingers, and all feel blessed.
Each rustle and rattle, a vibrant tune,
Under the warmth of the sun and the moon.

Melodies in the Meadow

In fields where daisies twirl and spin,
A bunny hops in, with a cheeky grin.
Fluffy clouds join in the ballet of fun,
As grasshoppers sing under warming sun.

The daisies sway, with rhythm so bright,
Telling tales of the day and the night.
A ladybug waltzes with breezy charms,
While butterflies flit with grace in their arms.

Bees buzz in chorus, a jittery tune,
Stealing a moment from afternoon.
They dance in circles, a sweet parade,
While the sun dips low, and shadows invade.

So grab a partner, and join the fun,
In this meadow where all is done.
Every creature from butterfly to bee,
Unites with laughter, wild and free.

Echoes of the Elderwood

In the heart of the woods, where shadows play,
The raccoons plan a mischief today.
Branches cackle while owls hoot loud,
As the forest gathers a quirky crowd.

Tiny creatures tiptoe on leaves,
Creating a concert that nobody leaves.
A fox chimes in with a clever rhyme,
As sunlight filters through, just in time.

Nuts roll and tumble in playful flight,
While squirrels giggle and dart out of sight.
Fungi dance, puffing out spores,
As laughter echoes through magical doors.

So slip in quietly, laugh with the trees,
Join the revelry, if you please.
In Elderwood's embrace, a melody grows,
A whimsical tale where anything goes.

Lullabies of Leaf and Limb

In the twilight hush, as the stars peek out,
A chorus of crickets begins to shout.
The leaves rustle gently as if to yawn,
Telling sleepy tales till the light of dawn.

A firefly flickers, a guiding light,
While a sleepy old owl hoots just right.
The wind hums low, in a slumber song,
Wrapping the forest in dreams all night long.

Hush now, dear critters, let dreams take flight,
As the moon croons softly, a soothing sight.
Bears snuggle close, in their cozy den,
While the stars wink down, then smile again.

So close your eyes, in this leafy embrace,
Where the woodland whispers of a gentle place.
And when the day breaks, with laughter anew,
The forest will greet you with joy and ado.

Sagas of Silent Grove

In the grove where whispers play,
A squirrel chats in bold array,
He tells tall tales of acorn wars,
While birds roll eyes 'neath leafy shores.

A raccoon dances on one leg,
Proclaiming victory with a beg,
The trees all laugh, they sway in cheer,
A village feast of bark and beer.

The foxes strut in double time,
While frogs compose a cheeky rhyme,
The elder tree, in roots so wise,
Advises all to wear disguise.

So in this grove where laughter flows,
The silliness is how it goes,
With every rustle, giggles sprout,
In stories shared, there's naught a doubt.

The Wildwood Waltz

In the wildwood, feet do twirl,
Where fungi dance and mushrooms whirl,
The hedgehogs don their finest hats,
While badgers play their jazzy spats.

The owls hoot tunes, quite out of tune,
As fireflies light the night like noon,
A hedgerow band strikes up a beat,
With flowers swaying, it's all quite neat.

Up in branches, the squirrels prance,
In sticky honey, do they dance,
The whole forest joins the jig,
As fading moonlight starts to gig.

So grab a friend or take a leap,
In wildwood's waltz, the joys run deep,
For in this realm of rhythmic cheer,
Laughter echoes, loud and clear.

Dreamscapes Beneath the Canopy

Beneath the leaves, where dreams take flight,
A snail regales the stars each night,
With tales of cheese and questionable quests,
While crickets strum on twigs as guests.

The owlets giggle at shadowed sights,
As mice compete in acorn fights,
A raccoon shows off his shiny prize,
But really it's just a pair of fries.

In corners where the moonbeams play,
A frog croaks songs of yesterday,
With every splash in marshy glades,
The humor blooms, like lilies' shades.

A tapestry of laughter grows,
In dreamscapes where the silly flows,
So gather round, both young and old,
To share the giggles life unfolds.

Sonnet of the Shadowed Glade

In shadowed glade where pranks abound,
The rabbits skitter, never found,
They sing of carrots, crisp and bright,
While owls roll eyes at their delight.

The hedgehogs scheme with cunning plans,
To swipe the corn from picnic fans,
They laugh and snicker, sly and spry,
As fireflies light the evening sky.

A turtle spins in perfect grace,
And wins the race, oh what a face!
The wisdom of slow, they always say,
Can leave the swifters in dismay.

So let us toast with cups of dew,
To mischief and mirth that feel brand new,
In nature's arms, a joyful spree,
A sonnet sung, forever free.

Starlit Serenades in Bark

Underneath the moon's bright laugh,
A squirrel plays a tiny sax,
While crickets sing a silly rhyme,
And trees join in with rustling facts.

The owls are busy telling jokes,
Their punchlines fly like acorn snacks,
As fireflies light up the stage,
In this wild, woods-born, merry max.

Each branch sways with a witty grin,
As nature's band takes center stage,
The toads croak choruses of cheer,
And worms request a funny page.

With laughter ringing through the leaves,
And gusts of wind that tickle toes,
A melody of whimsy reigns,
In this grove where humor grows.

Reflections in the Rustic Realm

In the shade of old oak trees,
The chickens play a game of chase,
While goats compose their latest hits,
And ducks parade with flair and grace.

A hedgehog strums a tiny lute,
The rhythm makes the daisies sway,
As rabbits tap their little feet,
To the beat of the barnyard play.

A cow joins in with mooing tunes,
Each note as smooth as butter spread,
While farmers laugh and take a peek,
At this concert of the misled.

With giggles echoing through the field,
The sun sets low on this delight,
A rustic realm of fluffy fun,
Where every creature sings goodnight.

Canvas of the Canopied Night

Beneath the sky of velvet hues,
A canvas drips with starlit winks,
The raccoons paint with sticky paws,
And crickets sketch with tiny blinks.

The fireflies dance in patterns bright,
As owls hoot jokes from their high perches,
While foxes strut in feathered hats,
And laughter spills from leafy churches.

A nightingale writes silly songs,
On branches swaying soft and low,
As hedgehogs laugh and share their tales,
Of how they did a funny show.

With every brushstroke of the night,
The forest fills with playful glee,
An artful mix of wit and charm,
In this gallery of harmony.

The Harmony of Hidden Hearth

In the glow of a cozy fire,
Where shadows dance in comic flair,
The rabbits roast their carrot pies,
While badgers set the tales to air.

A hedgehog flips some crispy snacks,
And giggles fill the ancient logs,
As owls share stories, wide-eyed,
Of mischief played on snoozy dogs.

Around the hearth, they laugh and cheer,
Each critter boasts a quirky yarn,
With tales of mishaps and wild chases,
In the glow that feels like yarn.

So raise a glass of berry juice,
And let the puns flow like warm light,
A harmony of funny friends,
As stars shine down to join the night.

Natural Narratives Among the Needle

In the gold of a sunbeam, a squirrel did dance,

He twirled and he leaped in a crazy prance.
His acorns were grateful, they clapped with glee,
As he juggled them wildly beneath a tall tree.

A rabbit watched closely, with ears standing high,
He bellowed with laughter, a chuckling sigh.
The fox crept on slowly, his eyes full of jest,
A trio of friends, both foolish and blessed.

A parakeet cawed with a note sharp and bright,
As the forest erupted in whimsical flight.
They chirped silly tunes, with no hint of dread,
While a bear joined the chorus, his belly widespread.

In whispers of leaves, the stories take flight,
Of mischief and madness, from morning till night.
Each branch tells a tale, as the laughter resounds,
Among echoes of nature, where joy knows no bounds.

Forest Fantasia

Deep in the woods where the shadows grow tall,

A hedgehog held court, and proclaimed, "Come one, come all!"
With a crown made of moss and a cape of fine leaves,
He commanded the dance, as the forest believes.

The owls hooted softly, exchanging a wink,
As a nimble young rabbit prepared for a drink.
With acorns as goblets, they raised merry cheer,
In a bustling bazaar that appeared once a year.

The mushrooms were grooving, all purple and green,
A dancing brigade like you've never seen.
The raccoons did tango, with style and flair,
While the trees watched in awe, swaying soft in the air.

With the moon shining bright, their fun burgeoned bold,
As stories were spun of the brave and the old.
In whimsical harmony, each critter did sing,
In a forest of laughter, where joy was the king.

The Music of Moonlit Mornings

At dawn's tender touch, the critters awoke,

To the melody sweet of a frog with a croak.
He plucked at the reeds, his stage set in dew,
While crickets kept time, with a rhythm so true.

A badger chimed in with a laugh and a jig,
His belly was round, and his steps were quite big.
The hedgehogs applauded with tiny small paws,
As the sun peeked through, without any flaws.

The bumblebees buzzed and joined in the spree,
As flowers all danced to a bright symphony.
The sun stretched its arms, warming all in sight,
Celebrating nature from morning till night.

With a wink and a grin, the melodies soared,
And the breeze carried whispers of praises adored.
In this funny ballet, all life joined the song,
In the chatter and laughter, where everyone belongs.

Dreams in the Distal Drizzle

In the shade of the rain, the puddles all gleamed,

A hedgehog skated by, and everyone screamed!
He slipped and he slid with an acorn on board,
While a butterfly giggled, feeling fully adored.

The clouds like a blanket, all gray and so puffy,
Gave the bear a chill, making his fur all fluffy.
He danced with the raindrops, as they plinked on his snout,
While a wily old raccoon laughed, boisterous and stout.

The otters revved up in their little canoe,
They splashed and they laughed, with mischief to brew.
With laughter like thunder filling the air,
Each drop wrote a story of joking and care.

As evening descended, they shared tales anew,
Of the wild rain ballet, where the giggles flew.
With joy in their hearts and a warmth in their chests,
In the drizzle's embrace, they felt truly blessed.

Legends on Leafy Pathways

In the forest, tales were spun,
Of squirrels racing just for fun.
They'd chatter, leap, and take their flight,
While acorns crunched beneath their might.

A wise old owl began to rhyme,
About the raccoon who stole some time.
With slippery paws and a crooked grin,
He'd swipe the snacks, and then he'd win!

The rabbits danced in silly rows,
With floppy ears and wiggly toes.
They hopped around like goofy clowns,
Wearing on their heads those leafy crowns.

And when the sunset painted gold,
The trees shared secrets, fresh and bold.
Laughter echoed through each branch,
As critters gathered for a chance.

The Tune of Tranquil Time

A chipmunk plays a tiny flute,
While turtles dance in their slow suit.
The sunbeam dances on the floor,
As Nature's choir sings galore.

A frog croaks out a silly tune,
As crickets join beneath the moon.
The fireflies flicker with delight,
In this amusing night so bright.

The hedgehogs roll with giggles loud,
Feeling proud, as if they bowed.
And all around, the fun won't stop,
With woodland creatures ready to hop.

Each melody wraps in the air,
Creating joy everywhere.
So let's embrace this humorous time,
With laughter echoing in every rhyme.

Verses Carried by the Wind

A breeze whistled a cheeky song,
Where beetles boogied all night long.
The leaves would rustle, laughing loud,
As shadows danced beneath the cloud.

An empty hat flew past my head,
With whispers of a cat who fled.
His tales of chases filled with glee,
While dodging dogs beneath the tree.

The butterflies wore gowns of cheer,
As they twirled about without a fear.
They teased a snail who took too long,
To reach the flower, shy and strong.

And on this playful, breezy trail,
The stories spread like a happy tale.
With every gust, a laugh would grow,
In every moment, joy would flow.

Woodland Waltz Under Moonlight

Under the stars, the critters swayed,
With little feet that never strayed.
A raccoon led, with a swoosh and spin,
While all around, the laughter began.

The mushrooms lit the forest floor,
As fireflies flickered, wanting more.
They twinkled on in their glowing suits,
While owls kept watch on dancing roots.

A bear joined in with a silly jig,
His paws were large, but his moves were big.
The forest thrummed with a joyful beat,
As whole creatures twirled on dainty feet.

And as the moon cast a gleaming light,
The woodland critters bade goodnight.
With memories bright, they whispered low,
Of waltzing nights where laughter flowed.

Ode to the Canopy's Embrace

In the trees, a squirrel leaps,
Bouncing high on branches' sweeps.
He chatters loudly, what a fan!
Declaring himself the king of the clan.

A leaf falls down with a gentle swoosh,
The squirrel dodges, in a hurried push.
He flips and flops like a seasoned pro,
Claiming victory with a final show.

Birds squawk tales of glorious feats,
While ants below march to their beats.
They gossip 'bout who had the best song,
In this leafy world where they all belong.

Each stir and rustle brings laughter here,
Nature's jesters, so full of cheer.
A dance of shadows, a playful chase,
In this leafy kingdom, they find their place.

Verses of the Verdant Realm

The hedgehog wears a very fine coat,
While frogs croon softly in musical note.
The flowers giggle, all dressed in hues,
As grasshoppers leap, sharing the news.

A stoat tells jokes to a wise old owl,
Who hoots with laughter, a surprising growl.
The sun slips down, the shadows sway,
In this green place, humor's on display.

Each rustle in bushes could lead to a jest,
Whether it's silly or simply the best.
With twigs as microphones, all sing along,
The forest alive with a whimsical song.

The mushrooms sway to a tune of delight,
While fireflies flicker, lighting the night.
In this lush world, joy takes the stage,
A realm of laughter at every age.

Folk Songs of the Forest Floor

A raccoon strums on his tiny guitar,
Wearing a hat and dreaming of stars.
The shadows dance to a rhythm so light,
As critters gather for a pleasant night.

The rabbits drum on the hollowed logs,
A band of misfits, singing with frogs.
Their melodies rise through the leafy expanse,
Inviting all creatures to join in the dance.

The hedgehogs shimmy, the mice tap their feet,
While the owls watch on, feeling the beat.
This forest is packed with tunes and cheer,
Each note a giggle, each laugh sincere.

The sun dips low, painting the sky,
With purple and orange, as the stars shy.
In this concert of critters, joy's never a bore,
A jolly affair on the forest floor.

The Currents of Gentle Shadows

Under canopies, whispers float,
As a chatty chipmunk takes note.
He shares his tales of bread and cheese,
Of picnic plunders with such ease.

The shadows twist, they dance and prance,
A dizzying waltz, enchanting chance.
As crickets chirp their evening song,
The night sneaks in, where all belong.

Fireflies glint like stars gone astray,
While beetles roll logs like they're made of clay.
The humor of Nature, funny and bold,
In this twilight realm, stories unfold.

A wise old tree chuckles with glee,
Watching the antics with lively decree.
In the dance of shadows, laughter will swell,
Creating a magic too bright to quell.

The Timber Tapestry

In the forest where trees wear hats,
Squirrels debate the best acrobat,
A woodpecker drummed a silly tune,
While rabbits laughed beneath the moon.

A log rolled by with a giggly squeak,
It tickles the toes of a shy little creek,
Leaves whisper jokes to tickle the pine,
As nature dances in a line.

The branches sway in a wobbly jig,
A bush shimmies, looking rather big,
Creatures gather for a grand old show,
With cheers and howls, let the fun flow!

A hammock strung between two trees,
Holds dreams of naps and a buzzing breeze,
With every swing, a chuckle is born,
In the timber world, there's never a thorn.

Harmonies of the Herbal Hearth

At the edge of a garden, herbs hum and sway,
Basil's got jokes, making thyme play,
Mint's sharp wit gives the petunias a grin,
While cilantro dances, the joyful twin.

A tomato burst out in a fit of glee,
"Why did the herb cross the road?" said he,
"To spice up the sides, don't you know?
Chili peppers laugh, stealing the show!"

Under the sun, cucumbers groove,
Radishes roll in a cheeky move,
As daisies chuckle, swaying with cheer,
The garden's a stage, with joy to endear.

A merry band of veggies, all in a row,
Playing their tunes in a radiant glow,
With each new dawn, they bicker and jest,
In this herbal hearth, laughter is best.

Nature's Choral Cadence

In the branches high, a choir sings bright,
Crickets strum strings, in the soft twilight,
A frog croaks out a comical tune,
While fireflies twinkle, like stars in June.

The raccoons join in, a slapstick act,
Wearing old hats, they make a pact,
To tell tales of nights filled with sweet fun,
As owls hoot laughter, 'til night is done.

A breeze whispers secrets to rustling leaves,
Tickling the nappers who rest like thieves,
With branches swaying, the laughter grows loud,
Nature takes pride, in her merry crowd.

As dawn breaks through, the giggles endure,
Crickets still chirp, in a joyous allure,
For every note sung in this woodland space,
Is a wild embrace of humor and grace.

The Soft Strum of Spruce

Beneath a spruce, the critters convene,
A rabbit wears glasses, a wise little bean,
A fox tells tales of his clumsy old flight,
While hedgehogs giggle, rolling in delight.

A gentle hum floats through the wood,
As playful shadows twist and brood,
With every strum of the flowering vine,
The air grows heavy with laughter so fine.

The squirrel juggles acorns, oh what a sight!
The world's a circus and they're full of might,
Each flip and tumble gets cheers, not a frown,
In the soft strum of spruce, they'll never drown.

As twilight descends, their antics will stay,
In the heart of the forest where they laugh and play,
With whispers of joy in the cool evening air,
Their fun-loving spirit is beyond compare.

Woven Whimsies in the Wind

In a breeze that waddles by,
A chicken danced, oh my!
With floppy feet and silly grin,
That feathered fool, he spun again.

Squirrels held a concert loud,
In the branches, oh so proud.
With acorn drums and nutty tunes,
They played all night beneath the moons.

A whispering maple made a joke,
While vines around began to poke.
They tickled leaves, the laughter spread,
As critters rolled, they laughed instead.

So let us twirl in this green place,
With giggles shared and merry faces.
For nature's tales, spun with glee,
A quirky world, come dance with me!

Echoing Euphony of Eucalypt

In the gum tree's sway, there's chat,
Of koalas draped, and looking fat.
A waltz of branches craves the scene,
While kookaburras laugh, they preen.

The sunlit leaves make cheeky sighs,
As lizards do their silly highs.
A parrot squawks a pun so bold,
Saying, "I knew you when you were cold!"

A billy goat plays the tuba there,
A note so flat, it broke the air.
He snorted twice and took a bow,
The crowd went wild; "More! More now!"

In the eucalypt's embrace so wide,
Nature's antics let joy collide.
With laughter shared, our spirits lift,
A tapestry of quirks, our gift.

Galaxies of Green and Gold

In the forest's heart, a fish did sing,
On a leafy stage, a lively fling.
With fins that flapped and tail that swirled,
'Twas the oddest sight in the known world!

A dandelion spun a yarn so grand,
About frogs who wear hats, oh isn't that bland?
They croaked on cue, a froggy band,
With winks and quirks, they took a stand.

Goldfinches donned their finest attire,
With jackets bright, they dazzled dire.
They gallivanted, oh what a sight,
With twirls and dips, pure delight!

In galaxies of green and gold,
Every critter's tale is bold.
So let's embrace this merry spree,
And laugh together, wild and free!

Legends of the Leafy Lattice

Under the canopy, a legend grew,
Of a turtle who danced, quite askew.
With shell adorned in sparkly stars,
He twirled through roots and leapfrogged cars.

A bushy-tailed friend, the rabbit sage,
Wrote scrolls of rhymes upon a page.
He told of squirrels who'd bake the pies,
And share them 'round, oh what a surprise!

A hedgehog took the stage on high,
With prickly puns, made laughter fly.
He juggled berries while on a spree,
Declared, "I'm spiky but never mean!"

In the lattice formed by leaves so wide,
Adventure thrives, nowhere to hide.
With every tale spun in delight,
Legends march forth, our hearts ignite!

Stanzas of Sunlit Spaces

In the park, a dog wore shades,
Chasing squirrels in silly parades.
Sun slipped through leaves, a radiant dance,
While kids in a circle perfected their prance.

A bee tried to buzz a sweet serenade,
But tripped on a petal, an unplanned charade.
Laughter erupted like popcorn in air,
As a pigeon declared himself king of the fair.

A cat on a branch, with a gaze so divine,
Spotted a dog and plotted a line.
A leap and a tumble, safe on the grass,
While humans all laughed, saying 'Oh, what a class!'

So here in this spot, with bright skies displayed,
Joy dances around in this sunlit parade.
With laughter so light, and moments so sweet,
Life's simple pleasures can't be beat!

Reverberations of the Whispering Woods

In the woods, a squirrel told jokes,
To a owl who just rolled her eyes, like blokes.
While trees giggled as breezes would flutter,
And rabbits danced, getting mud in their butter.

A fox joined with a grin, so sly,
Claiming he'd outsmarted a pie in the sky.
Crickets all chirped, tapping their feet,
While mushrooms chuckled, feeling the beat.

A group of raccoons held a night feast,
But the blueberries turned into a sticky beast.
They slipped and they slid, what a ruckus it made,
While fireflies glimmered, the grandest parade.

The merry woods echoed with laughter so clear,
Where even the whispers were filled with good cheer.
Nature's own symphony, funny and wild,
Dancing with joy like a mischievous child.

The Ballad of the Bedraggled Brush

In an artist's shed, paints splashed galore,
A brush sat sulking, tired of the score.
With hair all frayed from a wild, bumpy ride,
It dreamt of the canvas each night, and then sighed.

A palette scolded, 'Your colors are sad!'
'You're meant for masterpieces, no need to feel bad!'
But the brush just grumbled, 'I've lost all my flair,
Every stroke I make gives no one a scare.'

One day in a groove, a foolish cat leaped,
Knocking over cans, while the brush narrowly peeped.
With a splash and a flick, colors swirled bright,
The bristle found rhythm, oh what a sight!

Now a mural stretched wide, where nothing made sense,
And laughter erupted, it was too immense.
The brush learned a lesson, to embrace every hue,
Sometimes the silliest strokes make the best view!

Intonations in the Ivy

In a garden of green, ivy climbed high,
While daisies debated, as bumblebees fly.
Frogs croaked a tune with a bubbling laugh,
Each note made the daisies sway on their path.

A ladybug danced on a leaf full of glee,
Shouting, 'Join my conga, it's wild and free!'
While worms down below jived in their place,
With wiggles and squiggles, they set quite the pace.

A chattering chat of the birds up above,
Sang silly love songs with a twist of tough.
'Hey you down there, chewing on dirt,
You could team with us, but watch out for hurt!'

So ivy climbed onward, wearing a grin,
As the garden erupted, inviting the din.
With petals and laughter adorning the hue,
This tale of the green brought joy anew!

Rhapsody of Roots

In a garden where laughter grows,
The carrots sing and the onion goes.
With potatoes dressed in their best attire,
They dance around the garden fire.

The daisies giggle, the roses wink,
As the snails gather for a drink.
A beetroot wears a crown of leaves,
While the lettuce blows whispers through the eaves.

In the soil where secrets rhyme,
The worms compose a tune of prime.
With every squirm, they write a jest,
In earthen sheets, their verses rest.

So raise a glass to greens so fine,
For nature's wit is truly divine.
In every patch, a tale does sprout,
Join the revelry, let laughter out.

Harmonies Among the Branches

Under the canopy, laughter reigns,
Where squirrels tell the silliest chains.
A pigeon croons a silly refrain,
As the woodpeckers tap in rhythmic gain.

The leaves clap hands, they're quite a sight,
Doing cha-chas in morning light.
The chipmunks play a game of tag,
While the old oak stands with a laugh and brag.

A crow in a hat insists he's wise,
Swears he can solve the moon's disguise.
The bees buzz jokes, they're quite the jest,
While butterflies flutter in their best quest.

So sing with me, oh friends of the grove,
In nature's choir, we truly strove.
For in this realm of whimsy and cheer,
Every chuckle makes the sky clear.

Verses of the Verdant Veil

In a meadow where breezes peek,
The flowers gossip, oh what a peek!
With daisies rolling on the soft grass,
The sun's a jester, can't let time pass.

A dandelion wears a crown of fluff,
While lifts of laughter are never enough.
The frogs on lily pads hold a court,
In their froggy tongues, jokes they report.

The wind whispers secrets of fun and cheer,
As the squirrels spin tales for all to hear.
The butterflies chase after witty lines,
In this playful theater, where nature shines.

So dance with joy on this vibrant stage,
Every heartbeat turns the page.
In this ballet of whimsy and play,
Join the art, come what may!

The Treetop Conductor

A tree stands tall, with a leafy bow,
Conducting giggles from below somehow.
The squirrels tap toes on every limb,
While sparrows chirp in harmonious whim.

With branches swaying like a playful dance,
The sunlight beams in a cheerful glance.
A raccoon plays the triangle bright,
As the wind hums sweet through day and night.

Under this maestro, the forest sways,
Creating symphonies through leafy days.
With acorns dropping like applause from high,
The melody whispers, oh my, oh my!

So revel in nature's orchestral spree,
Where laughter and joy roam wild and free.
In this concert of green and good cheer,
Join the fun, it's all happening here!

Solstice Songs of the Sylvan

In the forest, critters dance,
Squirrels wear their finest pants.
Owls sing low, a jazzy tune,
While raccoons shuffle 'round the moon.

Pine trees giggle, branches shake,
A bear tries to bake a cake.
Mice in hats break out in cheer,
While shadows jump from here to there.

The sunbeams shine, they start to tease,
Tickling leaves in summer's breeze.
A lizard dons a party hat,
As frogs join in with their big splat.

So let the woodland revelry sway,
With laughter ringing through the day.
Nature's choir, a silly scene,
Where joy is felt and grass is green.

The Chime of Clusters

In the orchard, fruits a-jive,
Apples giggle, trying to thrive.
Pears are dancing side by side,
While grapes roll over—what a ride!

Cherries gossip with great flair,
Plums are twirling through the air.
Bananas sing a funny song,
Bouncing on the branches strong.

Cider dreams of sparkling cheer,
While nuts play drums, they gather near.
A pomegranate tops the show,
With seeds that scatter to and fro.

The farmer laughs at this charade,
As bees conduct their sweet parade.
A fruit fest that could never tire,
As laughter rolls like a bubbling fire.

Treetop Tales

Up in the canopies, what a sight,
A raccoon shares his latest fright.
His tail is stuck in a sticky trap,
While squirrels chuckle, give a clap.

A squirrel's prance, a pinecone's roll,
They dart and dash, that's their goal.
With hollow logs as their old homes,
They've even made up silly poems!

An owl declares, "Who's wise today?"
But all his wisdom seems astray.
For he forgot where he placed his food,
Now he's wearing a frown, not in the mood.

As twilight drapes a blanket slow,
The critters giggle, putting on a show.
With leafy laughter in the air,
These treetop tales, beyond compare.

Enigma of the Elders

The old trees whisper ancient lore,
But pine cones drop amidst the floor.
"What was that?" the elder sighs,
Guessing games with closed-set eyes.

Creepy shadows start to dance,
While sunset gives the world a chance.
The owls play poker, that's their delight,
Cheating's easy when it's night!

Mossy wisdom holds a riddle,
"Who made the grape play the fiddle?"
The answer lost in gusts of glee,
As the breeze hums loud, "Just let it be!"

So join the elders in their fun,
Their leafy games have just begun.
With laughter ringing in the air,
You'll find the truth is everywhere.

Lyrical Light in the Luminescent Leaves

In the breeze the whispers dance,
Leaves giggle in a shaky prance,
A squirrel drops nuts with great finesse,
While birds look on, they'll never guess.

The sun peeks through the leafy veil,
A shadowed thief, on a tiny trail,
A ladybug struts in a tiny coat,
All the insects cheer, they're afloat!

The ground is soft, like a plump old cheese,
One jump too high, and down they tease,
The grass joins in, a ticklish feat,
As tiny voices shout, "Oh, that's quite neat!"

While nature sings in matches and sounds,
The foundation shakes; joy abounds,
A tumbleweed rolls with a silly twirl,
It's all just fun in this leafy swirl!

Monologues of the Mature Maple

Oh, what a tale, this trunk so wide,
With knots and scars, in quiet pride,
The birds dive in with cheeky flair,
While squirrels pretend they do not care.

A dance of shadows spins on grass,
Leaves laugh as raindrops take a pass,
"Watch me spin!" a branch does shout,
As acorns drop— "Oh, watch out!"

The winds arrive to share a jest,
"Hold on tight, it's a leaf fest!"
Branches wiggle, wood creaks low,
"I've seen it all, and still, I glow!"

These talks with crickets at twilight's call,
A tree's own jokes, a stand-up hall,
Nature's laughter echoes wide,
As twilight fades, let joy abide!

Ink and Ivy

In a nook where the ivy sprawls,
A bard writes funny in chalky scrawls,
A tree sees scenes, and takes a look,
As rabbits hop around the book.

Scribbling lines, the quill takes flight,
A squirrel's antics, pure delight,
"Just turn the page!" the ivy pleads,
While ants gather round to read the deeds.

"Once I saw a crow dressed fine,
In a tiny coat, oh, what a line!
He cawed and danced, a sight to see,
And all of us laughed, from vine to tree!"

As chatter rises in leafy layers,
Puns and giggles, nature's players,
In every nook, in every twist,
With ink and ivy, none can resist!

Murmurs from the Mossy Mound

Down by the creek where the soft greens lie,
A mossy mound starts to sigh,
"Life's a giggle, a funny game,
It tickles us all, we're never the same!"

Frogs sing out from a darkened log,
"Join our chorus, don't be a fog!"
This mound speaks wise with a gentle grin,
"Oh hop along, let the fun begin!"

A snail moves slow with a curious glance,
"I've got my shell, just watch me dance!"
As spiders weave their webs of cheer,
Moss chuckles softly, "I'm glad you're here!"

Echoes of joy through the leafy haze,
A world of smiles in the sun's warm rays,
Murmurs of mirth abound all around,
On this mossy mount, fun's always found!

www.ingramcontent.com/pod-product-compliance
Lightning Source LLC
Chambersburg PA
CBHW051628160426
43209CB00004B/559